CLIL Readers

 Audio available

Antarctica: the world's wildest continent

written by
Noelle Yaney Child

Antarctica is like no other continent. It is a wild place. No people have settled there permanently. A few thousand scientists visit Antarctica every year. They live in research stations. Some are seasonal and only open during the summer months. Others are permanent and remain open all year.

At the bottom of the world

Antarctica is located at the South Pole. It is the coldest place on Earth. Even in summer the temperature, in most areas, is below freezing. One winter, scientists recorded a temperature of − 89°C.

Antarctica is also the driest and windiest continent. The air temperature is usually too cold for rain. Only a few centimetres of snow fall there each year. Scientists call the continent a 'cold desert'. Wind reaches speeds of 320 km/h, which makes the air feel even colder.

Ice covers most of the land. The ice has built up over thousands of years. In some places it is three kilometres thick. A few areas called 'dry valleys' are not covered by ice, they are bare rock. The islands of Antarctica are a little warmer than the mainland. On one island, a volcano sends clouds of steam into the freezing air.

Even the ocean around Antarctica is icy. The temperature of the water is barely above freezing. Enormous sheets of ice cover the water near the coast. Giant blocks of ice float further away from the shore. They are called 'icebergs'. Some icebergs are flat. Strong winds carve other icebergs into huge sculptures.

Seasons are unusual in Antarctica. The Sun does not rise and set there every day. For six months the South Pole faces towards the Sun, so the Sun never sets and it even shines at midnight. This is summer in Antarctica. During the rest of the year, the South Pole faces away from the Sun. This means the Sun never rises and the continent is dark for six months. This is winter in Antarctica.

Wildlife

Very few animals and plants can survive on land all year round in Antarctica. The land is too cold and dry for trees or large plants to grow. Some Antarctic plants are low, fuzzy mosses, others are hard, flat lichens. Lichens are simple plants that grow on the surface of rocks. The largest land animal that lives in Antarctica is an insect called the 'Antarctic midge'. It is about the size of a grain of rice!

Animals in the Antarctic live mainly in the ocean. Whales swim through the waves. Huge elephant seals zoom under the ice. Smaller seals bark warnings from the rocky shore. Strange fish swim through the icy waters. Some fish have special blood that keeps them from freezing.

Thousands of penguins waddle into the icy waters. They dive in and out of the sea. Thousands of birds nest along the coast in summer. Gulls and other sea birds fly through the blue sky. Loud bird calls fill the air with sound.

Challenges on the ice

People who visit Antarctica face many challenges. Just getting there is difficult and dangerous. Planes can be caught in sudden snowstorms called 'blizzards'. Blizzards can make it impossible for a pilot to see. Ships can become trapped in the icy sea. Ice is heavy and strong. It moves over the water. If a ship becomes trapped, the ice can crush it.

Once scientists reach Antarctica, they must protect themselves from the cold. They wear a lot of warm clothes. They eat a lot of food. The body uses food to make heat. There is no wood on Antarctica for campfires. When people camp there, body heat, clothing and equipment are the only things that keep them from freezing to death.

Visitors must also protect themselves from the Sun. Although the summer sunlight is not very warm, it is dangerous. Harmful rays from the Sun can burn the skin. The Ozone Layer around the Earth protects us from the harmful rays, but the layer is very thin over Antarctica. Many harmful rays reach the continent. People must wear sunscreen and dark sunglasses to protect their skin and eyes.

Even taking a walk in Antarctica can be risky. The ice moves slowly over the land. Deep cracks called 'crevasses' form in the ice. Some are hidden under the snow. People can fall into these crevasses by accident.

Living with so many challenges is stressful. People staying in Antarctica plan fun activities to reduce the stress. In some research stations, workers play music for each other or hold cooking contests. Sometimes they have fancy dress parties.

Sharing a continent

Antarctica is a world treasure. It is one of the last unexplored places on Earth. Scientists visit Antarctica to study things they cannot study anywhere else. Some study the special wildlife there. Others study the layers of ice. The ice contains clues about what the Earth was like long ago. Other scientists visit Antarctica to study outer space. Telescopes near the South Pole can see deeper into the universe than from anywhere else on Earth.

Antarctica is not owned by any nation. Instead, many nations share the entire continent. In 1959, twelve nations signed an agreement. The Antarctic Treaty promises that Antarctica will be shared peacefully. The treaty includes rules about how these nations will use Antarctica. The rules help to protect the environment. Today more than fifty nations, including Spain, participate in the Antarctic Treaty. They are working together to keep Antarctica as free from pollution as possible.